10 Arrows of Wisdom

Rewrite your Story

Unleash your Inner Warrior
Transform your Struggles into Strengths

Isha Gangrade

Qurate
qurateboooks.com

10 Arrows of Wisdom

Rewrite your Story

Unleash your Inner Warrior Transform your Struggles into Strengths

Isha Gangrade

Published in 2024

© Published by

Qurate Books Pvt. Ltd.
Goa 403523, India
www.quratebooks.com
Tel: 1800-210-6527, Email: info@quratebooks.com

ISBN: 978-93-58982-26-8

ALSO BY THE SAME AUTHOR

#1 Amazon Bestseller - King Raavan: Beyond the Myths, Unveiling a Noble Legacy

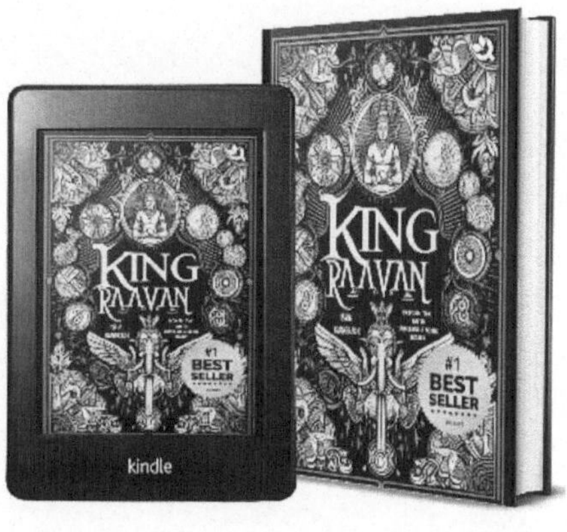

To my guiding light, my father:

Your wisdom, an eternal flame, illuminates my path. Though you've journeyed beyond, your spirit whispers in every word I write. In these pages, your legacy blooms anew. With each lesson shared, I feel your hand upon my shoulder, gently urging me forward, as you always did. This book is my heart's tribute to you— A constellation of memories, teachings, and love, Forever guiding those who seek wisdom in the darkness.

Contents

Preface

Hey there,

Welcome! Grab a seat, get at ease, and let's dive in together. Imagine we are putting out at a baseball game, cheering for our favourite group, or we are simply chilling over coffee, speaking about lifestyles. That's the vibe I need to bring to this book—friendly, comfortable, and real.

So, what is this book all approximately? Well, isn't life sometimes like a roller coaster? We as a whole have our promising and less promising times, and here and there, it seems like we're hitting a bigger number of lows than highs. You've come to the right place if you've ever been lost, stuck, or like you're always up against a wall.

We're approximately to embark on an adventure through the life of one of the maximum compelling characters from the Mahabharata—Karna. His story is full of classes which are as relevant these days as they have been centuries ago. Trust me, his struggles and triumphs can offer profound insights into our lives. Whether you're coping with identity issues, facing social stigma, navigating complex relationships, or trying to free up your capacity, Karna's life has something to educate us.

Let's be actual: lifestyles aren't always truthful. You might experience like you're constantly being dealt a lousy hand, going through barriers that appear now not viable to overcome. I've faced similar challenges and can relate to what you are enduring.

That's why I determined to prepare this book - to share what I've learned and with any luck offer some beneficial insights. I preferred to create something that felt like a conversation with a friend—someone who knows what you are going through and has a few solid recommendations to per cent.

We all face demanding situations that could make us revel in small, insignificant, or beaten. It could be the strain to suit right into sure mildew, the threshold of betrayal from someone you trusted, or the frustration of not accomplishing your entire capacity. These struggles can be paralyzing, making it hard to transport ahead.

Karna's tale is a treasure trove of knowledge. Despite being dealt a tough hand in lifestyle, he rose above his circumstances with courage, resilience, and integrity. By exploring his adventure, we can discover practical strategies to tackle our demanding situations.

I'm not just every other creator throwing recommendations at you. My debut book became an Amazon bestseller in 3 categories, and it is to readers such as you who discovered my approach relatable and useful. I've been through the wringer myself, and I've discovered lots alongside the manner. Now, I want to percentage those instructions with you.

By the end of this book, you'll have a toolkit of techniques that will help you:

- *Embrace your true identity and overcome emotions of inadequacy*
- *Build sturdy, trusting relationships while preserving your integrity*
- *Develop resilience to stand against lifestyle injustices and turn adversity into an increase*
- *Seek redemption and forgiveness, both from others and yourself*

These aren't simply summary concepts. The lessons in this book are drawn from actual lifestyle studies—each mine and Karna's. They're subsidized using centuries of wisdom and have helped infinite humans discover their manner via hard times. I promise that in case you take these classes to coronary heart and apply them in your lifestyles, you'll see a transformative alternate. You'll experience extra empowered, be more on top of things, and be more equipped to handle whatever lifestyles throw at you.

Life's too brief to stay stuck. Don't wait to begin making these changes. Dive into the primary chapter, and let's get started on this journey collectively. So, are you prepared to upward push above and rewrite your tale? Let's cross!

Now, turn to Next Page and let's begin this journey together.

Acknowledgments

Writing '10 Arrows of Wisdom' has been a transformative journey, made possible by the unwavering support of many incredible individuals.

To my family, whose love and patience sustained me through long writing sessions and moments of doubt. Your belief in me has been my anchor.

To my friends, who offered encouragement, laughter, and much- needed breaks. Your support kept me grounded and inspired.

To my dedicated beta readers, your feedback was invaluable in refining this work. Your insights helped shape each arrow of wisdom.

I'm deeply indebted to the timeless wisdom of the Mahabharata and its storytellers through the ages. This ancient epic continues to illuminate our modern lives.

Finally, to you, the reader - thank you for embarking on this journey of transformation. May these arrows of wisdom find their mark in your heart and help you unleash your inner warrior.

This book is a testament to the power of collective wisdom and support.

Thank you all for being part of this incredible adventure.

Section 1

Discovering Your True Self: How to Embrace Your Identity Without Feeling Lost Even If Society Says Otherwise

Welcome to Section 1, in which we embark on a journey of self-discovery and empowerment.

Do you ever feel like you're living your life for others, constantly trying to meet their expectations? What if there was a way to break free from this cycle and live authentically, embracing your true self? In this section, we'll explore the story of Karna, an ancient mythical hero who faced similar struggles. Despite being born into royalty, Karna experienced an ongoing internal battle as he grew up in a world that didn't fully accept him.

Through Karna's journey, we'll uncover valuable insights into our own lives and discover how to: Gain a deeper understanding of our true selves. Karna's story resonates with so many because it reflects the universal struggle of balancing personal identity with societal expectations. We may not be fighting battles with bows and arrows, but we face our own internal conflicts every day.

By examining the challenges Karna encountered and the choices he made, we can gain clarity on our own paths and find inspiration to overcome obstacles. Throughout this section, we'll explore various aspects of self-discovery and empowerment using Karna's journey as a guide. Here's what you can look forward to:

- ***Insights:** Practical tips and advice for making positive changes in your life.*
- ***Relatability:** Moments when you can acknowledge experiencing similar difficulties.*
- ***Hope:** Encouragement that you can find happiness and strength as you continue reading.*

Keep in mind this isn't just about mastering Karna's journey—it's about discovering your own path through his insights.

Are you ready to embark on this transformative voyage of self-discovery? If so, let's begin our journey together!

Chapter1

Facing Rejection: Rising Above the Caste Divide

"Your true identity is defined not by your circumstances, but by your determination to overcome them"

- Unknown

You know that sinking feeling—the one where you feel rejected, not good enough. Maybe it's a job you didn't get, a friendship that didn't work out, or something deeper. But what if that rejection could be the key to discovering who you truly are? The story of Karna, a legendary warrior from the Mahabharata, is all about overcoming adversity and embracing your unique identity. It's a story that resonates deeply, especially for those who've felt like they don't quite belong.

Imagine being born into royalty, destined for greatness, but then being abandoned by your own family because of your lineage. That's Karna's story. He faced rejection at every turn, yet he never gave up. He carried a fire within him, a spirit that refused to be extinguished.

Karna's journey teaches us that even when the world throws its worst at you, there's a strength inside that can lead you to self-acceptance and a fulfilling life. Karna's story is more than just battles and war; it's about discovering where you belong in a world that often misunderstands you. Although he was born into royalty, he was raised as the son of a charioteer. This constant clash of identities left him searching for validation from those around him.

Despite the numerous obstacles he encountered, Karna never lost sight of his true self. He remained steadfast in his principles and convictions, even when it meant challenging societal norms. Karna's tale serves as a powerful reminder that each of us possesses the ability to shape our journeys. We need not conform to society's expectations or allow our pasts to dictate our futures. Instead, we can wholeheartedly embrace our individuality and carve out our paths.

Discovering Your True Self Amidst Societal Expectations

A lot of us experience societal pressures like Karna which makes it difficult to know who we truly are. In this case, some people may have to follow prescribed paths or play defined roles leading to an identity crisis. The secret lies in self-realization.

Steps to Self-Discovery: Unleashing Your True Self

1. **Reflect on Your Values and Beliefs:** Dive deep into what truly matters to you. What are those deep-down beliefs that make you, well, you? Take a moment to scribble 'em down, and you'll see how they're like the building blocks of your very own personal brand, buddy.
2. **Discover Your Passions:** Engage in activities that ignite your soul. These passions reflect your true self. Embrace what brings you happiness and satisfaction.

3. **Seek Insights from Trusted Allies:** Ask your closest friends or mentors to point out your strengths and unique qualities. They can often recognize the best in you that you may miss.
4. **Embrace Solitude:** Allocate time in solitude to connect with your inner thoughts and emotions. This serene introspection aids in comprehending oneself devoid of external influences.

Karna often felt isolated and confused due to his dual identity. He was not entirely accepted by the royal house or the charioteers. To escape from such feelings, a person needs to develop inner resilience and faith in oneself.

1. **Practice Self-Compassion:** Be compassionate with yourself and admit that sometimes it is okay not to know where you are or what one is doing.
2. **Set Achievable Goals:** They can help boost your self-esteem and a sense of direction.
3. **Celebrate Your Achievements:** Whenever you achieve something, no matter how insignificant this might seem appreciate it.

Karna's journey was crucially defined by self-acceptance. He recognized who he was despite being disapproved by society and banked on his strengths. It encompasses accepting all aspects of oneself, including flaws and shortcomings.

Accepting yourself unconditionally is the only way to truly embrace your identity. In other words, it means no longer relying on others for validation but instead recognizing one's worth.

Karna's adventure shows that our unique identity must be embraced all the time. Through rejection and difficult moments, he stood firm on his principles and values. His experiences encourage us to stand proud and tall as individuals.

Turning Rejection into Strength

Rejection doesn't have to be the end of your story. Here are some steps to help you transform rejection into a source of strength:

1. **Reframe the Rejection:** View rejection not as a failure, but as a redirection. Karna faced numerous rejections, yet each one pushed him to hone his skills further and prove his worth. Similarly, you can see rejection as an opportunity to grow and find new paths.
2. **Build Resilience:** Just like Karna, building resilience is crucial. Resilience is the ability to bounce back from setbacks and keep moving forward. Studies have shown that resilient individuals are better at handling stress and are more likely to succeed in the long run.
3. **Seek Support:** Surround yourself with people who believe in you. Karna found support in unexpected places, such as his friendship with Duryodhana. While Duryodhana's motives were complex, his support gave Karna the validation he needed. Find your support system—friends, family, or mentors—who can provide encouragement and perspective.
4. **Focus on Self-Improvement:** Use rejection as a catalyst for self- improvement. Karna dedicated himself to becoming an unparalleled archer, despite being denied formal training. Identify areas where you can grow and invest in yourself.
5. **Stay True to Your Values:** Throughout his life, Karna remained true to his principles and values. Even when faced with immense pressure, he didn't compromise his integrity. In your journey, stay grounded in your values and let them guide your decisions.

As we conclude this chapter, remember that rejection is not the end— it's merely a detour on the road to your true potential. By drawing inspiration from Karna's journey, you can rise above rejection and embrace the possibilities that lie ahead. In the next chapter, we will explore how to build self-belief and conquer feelings of inadequacy, just like Karna did. Let's continue this journey together.

Turn the page, and let's dive into the next chapter, where we'll explore the power of self-belief and how to build unshakeable confidence, inspired by Karna's unwavering determination.

♦♦♦

Chapter 2

Conquering Inadequacy: Building Self-Belief Like Karna

"Believe you can, and you're halfway there."

- Theodore Roosevelt

Alright, so in our last chapter, we were hanging out with Karna as he experienced rejection and being looked down upon by society. We talked about how important it is to discover who you really are, be resilient, and learn to accept yourself. That's some good stuff, right?

Now that we've got that going for us, it's time to take it up a notch and tackle those feelings of not being good enough that can sometimes hold us back.

Karna's life was a constant combat against feelings of mediocrity, although he possessed extraordinary talents and had divine birth. Just imagine being an ultimate warrior in terms of strength and talent but one who is constantly told that he or she is not good enough due to their origin. This was the experience Karna underwent.

This moment where Karna becomes publicly humiliated for his non- royal blood status is especially touching in Mahabharata. Despite that, he never abandoned his dream. He set out to find the best teachers, went through countless difficulties, and perfected his abilities. For all of us, Karna's unshakeable faith in himself despite unending reproach remains instructive too.

At times, we all feel inadequate. It could be at work, in social settings, or even within our families. I recall a period during which I felt wholly inadequate. After I had published my first book, which was a bestseller, I was assailed by waves of self-doubt together with success. I always asked myself whether I was good enough, deserving of the accolades and whether I could match the expectations.

Karna always made me think in such times of self-doubt, how much he could manage facing heavy criticism but still carried on. His story helped me realise that feeling inadequate is a part of the journey, but it doesn't define our worth or potential.

Steps to Building Self-Belief

Building self-belief is a process, and just like Karna, we need to take actionable steps to reinforce our confidence. Here are some practical steps to help you build unshakable self-belief:

1. **Recognize Your Strengths:** Take a moment to think about your strengths and achievements and write them down. Karna knew what he was good at - his archery skills, his courage, and his unwavering loyalty. Similarly, acknowledging your own strengths can lay a solid foundation for self-belief.
2. **Daily Affirmations:** Repeat positive affirmations that boost your self- belief every morning.
3. **Skill Development:** Dedicate 15 minutes daily to develop a skill you're passionate about.

4. **Visualize Success:** Visualization is a powerful tool. Take a few minutes each day to visualize your success. Imagine yourself achieving your goals and basking in the sense of accomplishment. This mental exercise can significantly boost your confidence.
5. **Celebrate Wins:** Acknowledge and celebrate small victories to build confidence regularly.

By following these steps, you can gradually strengthen your self-belief, just like Karna did. Remember, building self-belief is a journey, so be patient with yourself and celebrate every step forward.

Personal Experience: Overcoming Personal Doubts

Let me share a personal story. When I started writing my second book, the pressure of repeating the success of my first bestseller was overwhelming. I doubted my abilities and feared failure. However, I remembered Karna's resilience and decided to take actionable steps to build my self-belief.

I began by acknowledging my strengths as a writer, setting achievable writing goals, and seeking feedback from trusted peers. I practised self- compassion, reminding myself that it's okay to feel doubt but not to be defined by it. Visualization became a daily ritual, helping me see the success I wanted to achieve. These steps transformed my mindset, and I wrote with newfound confidence.

As we conclude this chapter, remember that building self-belief is a journey, not a destination. By taking actionable steps inspired by Karna's story, you can conquer feelings of inadequacy and unlock your true potential. In the next chapter, we will explore the power of embracing your unique identity and how to integrate different aspects of yourself without losing who you are. Let's continue this transformative journey together.

Turn the page, and let's dive into the next chapter, where we'll explore how to embrace your unique identity, inspired by Karna's unwavering determination to stay true to himself despite the odds.

♦♦♦

Chapter 3

Embracing Your Unique Identity: Lessons from Karna

"To be yourself in a world that is constantly trying to make you something else is the greatest accomplishment."

- Ralph Waldo Emerson

In the previous chapter, we focused on building self-belief. We discovered how Karna had an unbending self-belief despite his feelings of inferiority and external censure. We also discussed practical measures like acknowledging strengths, appropriating goals and seeking positive compliments. I hope you have had time to implement these steps because a foundation of consideration is essential as we go ahead.

Karna's life was an incessant fight for him to express himself. He observed the social expectations imposed on him by those dynasties. Despite this, however, Karna remained true to himself. He was firm in his values and ideas and refused society to tell him who he could be.

When Karna's low social status gets him excluded from a prestigious archery tournament, a moment of great power manifests itself. Instead of giving up in despair, Karna uses his powers to surpass even the privileged prince Arjuna and proves to be an exceptional archer and his story gives us valuable lessons on the importance of knowing ourselves and being true to ourselves, regardless of external challenges.

Personal Experience:

Raised in Indore, the heart of Madhya Pradesh, I grew up amidst a good atmosphere and the acceptance shown by that community. I moved to Chennai post-pandemic. Often, I felt that I was an outsider in the workplace. My colleagues would sometimes remind me indirectly and directly that I wasn't one of them, maybe for the differences in language, variance in culture, and even food differentials or preferences.

There were days when these differences seemed too much to bear. Some colleagues made it very difficult to work, questioning my abilities and undermining my efforts. It was a harsh and lonely experience; however, I found strength in Karna's story. Much like the rejected Karna who rose above the rejection, I chose to focus on my work and my capabilities.

I continued working hard, and slowly the proof was there in my works. Soon, most of my efforts began to bear fruit; my contributions became recognized, and I started to establish myself. Thus, within what once felt like an environment set on destroying me, I realized the power of truly accepting myself.

Embracing Your Unique Identity

Understanding and embracing your unique identity can be challenging, especially in a world that often tries to fit you into predefined molds. Here are some action steps you can implement right away:

1. **Identify Your Core Values:** Your values are the foundation of your identity. Take some time to reflect on what truly matters to you. Is it honesty, compassion, creativity, or something else? Write down your core values and consider how they influence your decisions and actions.
2. **Celebrate Your Uniqueness:** Recognize and celebrate what makes you different. Just as Karna celebrated his unique skills and strengths, you should acknowledge the qualities that set you apart. These differences are your greatest assets.
3. **Stay Authentic:** In a world that constantly tries to change you, staying authentic can be a powerful statement. Karna stayed true to his principles, even when it was difficult. Embrace authenticity by being honest with yourself and others about who you are and what you stand for.
4. **Set Boundaries:** Setting boundaries is crucial for maintaining your identity. Know your limits and communicate them clearly to others. Boundaries help protect your values and ensure that you're not compromising your identity to please others.
5. **Seek Support:** Surround yourself with people who appreciate and respect your unique identity. Karna found support in Duryodhana, who valued his skills and potential. Find your support system—friends, family, or mentors who encourage you to be your true self.

At this point, you might be feeling a bit overwhelmed. Embracing your unique identity and staying true to yourself is not an easy task. Remember, to focus on one step at a time. Embracing your identity is a journey, not a sprint. Make sure to take care of your physical and emotional well-being. This will help you stay balanced and focused

As we wrap up this chapter, remember that embracing your unique identity is a powerful journey that requires self-awareness and courage. By drawing inspiration from Karna's unwavering determination to stay true to himself, you can navigate societal pressures and stay authentic. In the next chapter, we will explore how to balance different aspects of your identity without losing yourself. Let's continue this journey together.

Turn the page, and let's dive into the next chapter, where we'll explore the art of balancing different aspects of your identity, inspired by Karna's ability to integrate his multifaceted life.

♦♦♦

Chapter 4

Balancing Different Aspects of Identity: Integrating Multiple Identities Without Losing Yourself

"To thine own self be true, and it must follow, as the night the day, thou canst not then be false to any man."

- William Shakespeare

In the last chapter, we focused on embracing your unique identity. We explored how to identify your core values, celebrate what makes you unique, stay authentic, set boundaries, and seek support. I hope you've taken some time to reflect on your core values and started celebrating your unique qualities. Remember, these steps are crucial in building a strong sense of self.

Karna's life was a complex interplay of multiple identities. Born a prince, raised as a charioteer's son, and later becoming a king, his journey was anything but straightforward. He had to constantly balance these different aspects of his identity without losing his true self. Despite the conflicting roles and societal expectations, Karna managed to integrate his multifaceted life by staying true to his core values and principles.

There's a powerful moment in Karna's story where he accepts his true lineage but chooses to remain loyal to his adoptive family and friend Duryodhana. This decision illustrates his ability to balance different aspects of his identity while staying true to his sense of loyalty and honor.

Karna's journey teaches us that it's possible to integrate various facets of our identity without losing ourselves.

Balancing Different Aspects of Identity

Balancing different aspects of your identity can be challenging, especially when you feel pulled in multiple directions by societal expectations, family roles, and personal aspirations. Here are some steps to help you navigate this complex process:

1. **Acknowledge all parts of yourself :** Accept every aspect of who you are, even if they appear contradictory. Recognizing all aspects of yourself develops a more integrated and harmonious personality, like Karna did with his regal pedigree and charioteer upbringing.
2. **Prioritize your values :** Let your primary values guide your decisions and actions. When it comes to defining yourself, your values should serve as a guidepost. Karna's steadfast dedication and honor enabled him to traverse his varied existence.
3. **Be Adaptable:** Life is dynamic, and so are our identities. Be open to change and willing to adapt as you grow and evolve. Embrace new roles and let go of those that no longer serve you.
4. **Seek Harmony,** Not Perfection: Look for methods to align diverse components of your identity. Aim for harmony rather than perfection. It's okay if some roles

occasionally take precedence over others. The goal is to create a balanced and fulfilling life, not a flawless one.

5. **Practice self-reflection:** Take time each day to consider how effectively you're balancing different components of your identity. This allows you to be loyal to yourself and make the required changes. Karna's self-reflection helped him to adhere to his convictions despite the external influences.

Personal Experience: Balancing Work and Personal Passion

Balancing my career and passion for writing has been a challenge. As a Quality Analyst, my job requires precision and analysis, contrasting with the creativity and emotional depth needed for storytelling. Initially, work consumed most of my time, leaving little for writing. However, I realized that both are essential to my identity.

To balance them, I dedicated time for writing, adjusting my schedule as needed. I infused storytelling into work presentations, enhancing engagement and performance. Setting clear boundaries between work and writing time helped me focus and be productive in both areas.

This journey taught me to aim for harmony, not perfection. It's fine for one role to take precedence at times, as long as there's overall balance. Integrating my professional life with my writing passion has enriched my identity.

As we conclude this chapter, remember that balancing different aspects of your identity is an ongoing journey. By drawing inspiration from Karna's ability to integrate his multifaceted life, you can navigate societal pressures and stay true to yourself. In the next chapter, we will explore the role of self-acceptance in resolving an identity crisis and embracing your true self. Let's continue this transformative journey together.

Turn the page, and let's dive into the next chapter, where we'll explore the power of self-acceptance and how it can help you resolve identity crises and embrace your true self, inspired by Karna's journey.

♦♦♦

Section 2

Navigating Relationships and Family: How to Build Trust and Loyalty Without Getting Hurt Even If You've Been Betrayed Before

Great job on getting to this big milestone!

You've grasped the fundamentals of understanding yourself, found your strengths, and discovered the way to integrate numerous factors of yourself in a harmonious way. You've demonstrated sturdy dedication and effort, and you've got every reason to experience very proud of your achievements.

Next, we'll have a look at the more precise aspects of relationships and own family life. In this component, we'll discuss the complicated issues of accept as true with and loyalty, specially while there are issues like betrayal and arguments.

In this part, we will examine the intricacies of trust and loyalty, particularly when relationships face challenges such as betrayal and conflict. Relationships are essential in our human experience, and knowing how to establish and sustain healthy, reliable connections is vital for personal development and satisfaction.

Each chapter in this section aims to delve further into helping you comprehend and enhance your relationships. Reading Karna's story isn't only for entertainment, but also for applying its timeless lessons to your own life.

At the conclusion of this section, you will have a better grasp on how to handle intricate relationships with trust and honesty. You will receive the necessary tools to:

1. *Address family conflicts*
2. *Establish lasting friendships*
3. *Uphold loyalty while staying true to your beliefs*

Are you prepared to strengthen your relationships and create lasting bonds? Let's jump in and begin this journey of transformation side by side. You are just a few pages away from discovering the best version of your relational self.

Chapter 5

The Power of Self-Acceptance: Embracing Your True Self

"Accept yourself, love yourself, and keep moving forward. If you want to fly, you have to give up what weighs you down."

- Roy T. Bennett

In the last chapter, we focused on balancing different aspects of your identity. We learned from Karna's journey how to acknowledge all parts of ourselves, prioritize our values, communicate clearly, create harmony, and practice self-reflection. Remember, maintaining balance is an ongoing journey.

Self-acceptance begins with acknowledging and embracing all aspects of yourself - the strengths, weaknesses, quirks, and imperfections. It's about nurturing self-compassion and understanding that everyone, including yourself, is a work in progress. Karna's life was filled with constant reminders of his social status and lineage. Despite his skills and valor, he was often reminded that he was not "truly" a prince. Yet, Karna reached a point where he accepted his identity, with all its complexities and contradictions. This self-acceptance did not come easily but was a result of deep reflection and resilience.

Karna's encounter with his birth mother, Kunti, was a pivotal moment in his story. Upon learning his true lineage, Karna grappled with a significant identity crisis. While he had the option to leave his past behind and unite with his birth family, he opted to stay true to those who had brought him up and his dear friend Duryodhana. This choice underscored Karna's acknowledgement of his complex identity and his steadfast dedication to his principles.

Case Study

Research indicates that individuals practicing self-acceptance tend to enjoy greater psychological well-being and resilience. For instance, research suggests that accepting one's imperfections can lead to healthier relationships and more effective coping with life's adversities.

The Role of Self-Acceptance in Resolving an Identity Crisis

Self-acceptance is the foundation of a strong and authentic identity. It allows you to embrace all parts of yourself, including your flaws and imperfections, and to live a life that is true to your values and beliefs. Here are some steps to help you embrace self-acceptance:

1. **Acknowledge Your Flaws and Imperfections:** Everyone has flaws and imperfections. Acknowledging them is the first step towards self- acceptance. Karna accepted his limitations and used them as a motivation to improve himself rather than as a source of self-doubt.

2. **Forgive Yourself:** Forgive yourself for past mistakes and shortcomings. Holding onto guilt and regret can prevent you from moving forward. Karna faced numerous setbacks, but he didn't let them define his future.
3. **Celebrate Your Achievements:** Take time to celebrate your achievements, no matter how small they may seem. This will help reinforce a positive self-image. Karna celebrated his victories and used them as a reminder of his capabilities.
4. **Practice Self-Compassion:** Be kind to yourself, especially during challenging times. Practicing self-compassion can help you stay resilient and maintain a positive outlook. Karna's self-compassion allowed him to remain strong in the face of adversity.
5. **Live Authentically:** Living authentically means being true to yourself and your values, even when it's difficult. Karna's decision to stay true to his upbringing and values, despite knowing his royal lineage, is a powerful example of living authentically.

You've made incredible progress on this journey of self-discovery and self-belief. Embracing your unique identity and balancing its different aspects is no small feat. Remember to acknowledge your progress and stay focused on the journey ahead and celebrate each step forward. Keep engaging with your support system. Share your successes and challenges with them.

As we conclude this chapter, remember that self-acceptance is a powerful tool for resolving identity crises and embracing your true self. By drawing inspiration from Karna's journey, you can learn to accept all parts of yourself and live a life that is true to your values. In the next chapter, we will explore the role of resilience in overcoming life's challenges and how to build emotional strength, inspired by Karna's unwavering determination. Let's continue this transformative journey together.

Turn the page, and let's dive into the next chapter, where we'll explore the power of resilience and how to build emotional strength to overcome life's challenges, drawing inspiration from Karna's remarkable journey.

♦♦♦

Chapter 6

Trust Issues: Building Healthy Relationships

"Trust is the glue of life. It's the most essential ingredient in effective communication. It's the foundational principle that holds all relationships."

- Stephen Covey

In the previous chapter, we focused on the power of self-acceptance. We explored how to acknowledge our flaws, forgive ourselves, celebrate achievements, practice self-compassion, and live authentically. Remember, self-acceptance is the cornerstone of building healthy relationships.

Karna's life was a testament to the complexities of trust and loyalty. Despite being rejected and humiliated by society, he found an unlikely friend in Duryodhana, the prince of the Kauravas. Duryodhana saw Karna's potential and offered him unwavering support and friendship. In return, Karna's loyalty to Duryodhana was absolute, even when it led him into morally ambiguous situations.

One striking example of Karna's loyalty is his decision to stand by Duryodhana during the great war of Kurukshetra, despite knowing that his true brothers were on the opposing side. This unwavering loyalty demonstrated Karna's deep sense of trust and commitment, even in the face of tremendous personal conflict. While Karna's story highlights the strength of loyalty, it also serves as a cautionary tale about the importance of discernment in trust.

Building Healthy Relationships Based on Trust

Building healthy relationships requires a strong foundation of trust. Here are some steps to help you build and maintain trust in your relationships:

1. **Be Honest and Transparent:** Honesty is the bedrock of trust. Be open and transparent with your intentions, feelings, and actions. Karna's relationship with Duryodhana was built on mutual honesty and respect, which solidified their bond.
2. **Communicate Effectively:** Effective communication involves both speaking and listening. Make an effort to listen actively and empathetically. When you communicate clearly and openly, you reduce misunderstandings and build stronger connections.
3. **Show Consistency and Reliability:** Trust is built through consistent and reliable actions. Be dependable and follow through on your commitments. Karna's loyalty to Duryodhana was unwavering, which demonstrated his reliability.
4. **Respect Boundaries:** Respecting personal boundaries is crucial for maintaining trust. Understand and honor the limits of others, and communicate your own boundaries clearly.

5. **Seek Forgiveness and Make Amends:** When trust is broken, seek forgiveness and make amends. Acknowledge your mistakes, apologize sincerely, and take steps to rebuild trust. Karna faced many challenges, but his ability to seek forgiveness and remain loyal helped him maintain relationships.

Case Study: The Power of Trust in Teamwork

Consider the story of a high-performing team at a leading tech company. The team had diverse skills and backgrounds, but what set them apart was their trust in one another. Each team member was honest about their capabilities and limitations, communicated openly, and respected each other's boundaries. When mistakes were made, they were addressed promptly and constructively. This trust enabled them to collaborate effectively, innovate, and achieve remarkable success.

Research Findings: Trust and Relationship Satisfaction

Research has consistently shown that trust is a key predictor of relationship satisfaction. A study published in the Journal of Social and Personal Relationships found that individuals who reported higher levels of trust in their partners also reported greater relationship satisfaction and commitment. Trust fosters a sense of security and belonging, which is essential for healthy relationships.

As we conclude this chapter, remember that building healthy relationships based on trust is an ongoing journey. By drawing inspiration from Karna's loyalty and commitment, you can navigate the complexities of trust and strengthen your connections. In the next chapter, we will explore the dynamics of friendship and how to balance loyalty with personal integrity. Let's continue this transformative journey together.

Turn the page, and let's dive into the next chapter, where we'll explore the dynamics of friendship and how to balance loyalty with personal integrity, drawing inspiration from Karna's unwavering commitment to his friends and values.

♦♦♦

Chapter 7

Friendship Dynamics: Balancing Loyalty and Integrity

"Friendship is born at that moment when one person says to another, 'What! You too? I thought I was the only one."

- C.S. Lewis

In the previous chapter, we delved into the importance of trust in building healthy relationships. We explored how honesty, effective communication, consistency, respecting boundaries, and seeking forgiveness can help establish and maintain trust. Remember, trust is the glue that holds relationships together.

Karna's life was profoundly shaped by his friendship with Duryodhana. This relationship was rooted in mutual respect and unwavering loyalty. Despite societal rejection and the complexities of their circumstances, Duryodhana saw Karna's potential and offered him the support and recognition he had long been denied. In return, Karna's loyalty to Duryodhana was absolute, even when it placed him in morally challenging situations.

One of the most poignant examples of Karna's loyalty is his decision to support Duryodhana during the great war of Kurukshetra, despite knowing that his true brothers were on the opposing side. This unwavering loyalty demonstrated Karna's deep sense of friendship and commitment, but it also highlights the importance of balancing loyalty with personal integrity. While Karna's loyalty was commendable, it serves as a reminder of the complexities and potential conflicts inherent in friendships.

Balancing Loyalty and Integrity in Friendships Research

Navigating the dynamics of friendship requires a delicate balance between loyalty and personal integrity. Here are some steps to help you maintain this balance:

1. **Define Your Values:** Clearly define your values and let them guide your actions and decisions. Karna's unwavering loyalty to Duryodhana was rooted in his values of gratitude and honor. Similarly, understanding your core values will help you navigate complex friendship dynamics.
2. **Communicate Openly:** Open communication is crucial for maintaining trust and integrity in friendships. Be honest about your feelings and concerns. Karna's open communication with Duryodhana about his loyalty and intentions strengthened their bond.
3. **Set Healthy Boundaries:** Establishing and respecting boundaries is essential for maintaining a healthy balance between loyalty and integrity. Boundaries help protect your values and ensure that your loyalty does not compromise your principles.
4. **Evaluate the Impact of Your Actions:** Consider the potential impact of your actions on both your friend

and your own integrity. Karna's decision to support Duryodhana had significant consequences for both his friendship and his moral standing. Reflecting on the implications of your choices can help you make more balanced decisions.

5. **Seek Balance in Loyalty:** Loyalty should not come at the expense of your integrity. Strive to find a balance where you can support your friends while staying true to your values. This balance will ensure that your loyalty is both genuine and sustainable.

Case Study: Balancing Loyalty and Integrity in Professional Relationships

Consider the story of a manager named Sarah who faced a dilemma at work. She had a close friendship with a colleague, Mark, who was struggling with his performance. While Sarah wanted to support Mark, she also needed to maintain her professional integrity and the team's productivity.

Sarah decided to have an open and honest conversation with Mark. She expressed her concerns about his performance while also offering her support and resources to help him improve. By setting clear boundaries and communicating openly, Sarah was able to balance her loyalty to Mark with her professional integrity, ultimately strengthening their friendship and improving team dynamics.

Research Findings: The Role of Integrity in Friendships

Research has shown that integrity is a key component of healthy and lasting friendships. A study published in the Journal of Personality and Social Psychology found that friendships based on shared values and mutual respect were more likely to endure and provide emotional support. Integrity fosters trust and respect, which are essential for maintaining strong friendships.

As we conclude this chapter, remember that balancing loyalty and integrity is essential for maintaining healthy and fulfilling friendships. By drawing inspiration from Karna's unwavering commitment to his friends and values, you can navigate complex friendship dynamics and build stronger, more authentic connections. In the next chapter, we will explore the role of family relationships, how to resolve conflicts, and how to heal past wounds. Let's continue this transformative journey together.

Turn the page, and let's dive into the next chapter, where we'll explore the complexities of family relationships and how to resolve conflicts and heal past wounds, drawing inspiration from Karna's interactions with his family.

♦♦♦

Chapter 8

Family Tensions: Healing Through Understanding

"Family is the compass that guides us. They are the inspiration to reach great heights, and our comfort when we occasionally falter."

- Brad Henry

In the previous chapter, We examined the importance of empathy and more heavily developed relationships. You were asked to invest in active listening and open communication with those in your life. Make sure you have worked on strengthening your empathy and having meaningful conversations with others before you began reading this chapter. Remember, the strength of your family relationships can be a powerful support as you pursue your personal ambitions.

Karna, the renowned warrior of the Mahabharata, faced significant family conflicts from birth. Born to Kunti before her marriage, Karna was abandoned and brought up by a charioteer's family. This clandestine beginning planted seeds of tension that persisted. Discovering his true lineage left Karna torn between loyalty to his adoptive family and his newfound biological heritage.

Karna's life illustrates the trials of familial discord. Despite his awareness of his true identity, he stayed faithful to Duryodhana, who embraced him in rejection by others. Karna's embracing of his intricate family bonds, while upholding his principles and allegiance, imparts a profound lesson in navigating family conflicts.

Personal Experience

Family tensions can be terribly troublesome and therefore very emotionally draining. When I was a little boy, my family experienced quite a tiff, composite of misunderstandings and unvoiced grievances. It took years to realize that each of us was fighting his own demons and that it was understanding someone's situation was going to heal it. Over time, with increased trust through the gradual sharing of our thoughts and feelings, we were able to mend relations and build a good supportive family.

In another example, I watched an understanding-based change take place in my best friend's relationship with her mother. In her late twenties, this daughter had always been at loggerheads with her mother over her professional choices and lifestyle differences. But when both chose to bring understanding into their disagreements, their relationship thrived. By that time, the mother became more sensitive to her daughter's dreams, and the daughter learned to appreciate her mom's wise and caring attitude. This reparation not only restored their relationship but strengthened it even more.

Action Steps

Understanding and healing family tensions require empathy, active listening, and a willingness to see things from the other person's perspective. It's about finding common ground and acknowledging that each family member's feelings and experiences are valid. This approach fosters an environment of respect and open communication, which are essential for resolving conflicts and strengthening family ties.

1. **Practice Active Listening:** When a family member speaks, listen without interrupting. Show that you value their perspective.
2. **Empathy Exercise:** Put yourself in the shoes of the family member you have tension with. Write down how they might be feeling and why.
3. **Regular Family Check-Ins:** Schedule regular times to discuss any issues openly and calmly, ensuring everyone has a chance to speak.

Case Study

Research conducted by Dr. John Gottman, a renowned psychologist, highlights the significance of understanding and empathy in resolving family conflicts. His studies have shown that families who engage in open and empathetic communication tend to have stronger relationships and are better equipped to handle disputes constructively. For instance, families that participate in regular "family meetings" to discuss issues openly often report higher levels of satisfaction and cohesion.

As you move closer to the end of this journey, remember that the process of healing and understanding in family relationships is ongoing. Each step you take brings you closer to a harmonious and supportive family environment. Keep practicing empathy and open communication, and you'll continue to see positive changes.

In the next section, we will explore the role of resilience and redemption in overcoming life's challenges and achieving personal growth, inspired by Karna's remarkable journey. Let's continue this transformative journey together.

Turn the page, and let's dive into the next section, where we'll explore the power of resilience and redemption, and how to overcome life's challenges to achieve personal growth, drawing inspiration from Karna's inspiring story.

♦♦♦

Section 3

Unlocking Potential and Ambition: How to Achieve Your Dreams Without Compromising Integrity Even If the Odds Are Against You

Kudos to you for getting this far!

You have demonstrated so much determination and tenacity in engaging the complexities of self-discovery, relationship cultivation, and loyalty versus integrity. You have traveled the path, gathered some quick wins, and know more precisely where you stand along the way. Now as we get into the next real critical stage, the need is to tap one's true potential and chase one's dreams without compromising on one's integrity at any point in time when the odds are against one.

This section is about becoming the steamroller that busts the walls that give life limits, while consistently being true to your convictions and sailing high to your wishes. Every chapter of the section is meant to inspire you with related stories, contemporaneous advice, and actionable steps that will help unleash your potential and go after your ambitions with integrity. By the end of this section, you will truly possess a much better understanding of exactly how to break through some of the barriers, remain persistent, believe in yourself, and maintain a sound balance among your ambitions and your values.

Already, you have shown to be so resilient and very committed to reach this far. The insights and tools that will come in the subsequent chapters will enable you to chart your course effectively through the intricacies of ambition and integrity, so that your journey toward living your dreams is both successful and ethically sound.

Let's dive into the final stretch of this transformative journey together. The best version of yourself is just a few pages away.

Let's continue to break barriers, rise above limitations, and achieve our dreams without compromising our integrity. Flip the page, and let's begin Chapter 9, where we'll explore how to break barriers and unleash your true potential, inspired by Karna's remarkable journey.

Chapter 9

Breaking Barriers: Unleashing Your True Potential

"The only limit to our realization of tomorrow will be our doubts of today."

- Franklin D. Roosevelt

In the previous chapter, we explored the delicate balance between ambition and morality, learning from Karna's journey how to pursue our dreams without compromising our values. By now, you should have reflected on your ethical boundaries, aligned your goals with your values, and practiced self-reflection to ensure your actions remain true to your principles. I hope you've found the steps useful and have begun to see the positive impact of these practices in your life.

Karna's life was marked by numerous barriers—social status, lack of recognition, and constant rejection. Despite these obstacles, Karna refused to be confined by societal limitations. His determination to unleash his true potential was evident in his relentless pursuit of excellence, particularly in the field of archery.

One of the most significant moments in Karna's journey was his decision to seek training from Parashurama, the revered teacher of martial arts. Knowing that Parashurama only taught Brahmins, Karna disguised himself as one to gain the skills he needed. This decision, though ethically complex, showcased Karna's determination to break through societal barriers to achieve his goals.

Karna's perseverance paid off. He became one of the greatest archers of his time, earning respect and recognition despite the initial obstacles. His story is a powerful reminder that our potential is not limited by external circumstances but by our willingness to push through barriers and stay committed to our goals.

How to Break Barriers and Unleash Your True Potential

Breaking barriers and unleashing your true potential involves identifying the obstacles in your path and developing strategies to overcome them. Here are some steps to help you on this journey:

1. **Identify Your Barriers:** The first step in breaking barriers is to identify what's holding you back. These barriers can be external, such as societal expectations or lack of resources, or internal, such as self-doubt and fear. Make a list of the barriers you face and categorize them into external and internal obstacles.
2. **Set Clear Goals:** Having clear, achievable goals gives you a direction to channel your energy. Karna's goal was to become a master archer, which guided his actions and decisions. Set specific, measurable, achievable, relevant, and time-bound (SMART) goals that align with your ambitions.

3. **Develop a Plan of Action:** Create a detailed plan to overcome each barrier. This plan should include the steps you need to take, the resources you need, and the support systems you can rely on. For example, if lack of resources is a barrier, your plan might include finding scholarships, mentors, or other financial aids.
4. **Cultivate Resilience:** Resilience is the ability to bounce back from setbacks. Karna faced numerous rejections and challenges but remained resilient. Cultivate resilience by staying positive, learning from failures, and keeping a growth mindset. Remember, every setback is an opportunity to learn and grow.
5. **Seek Support:** Surround yourself with people who support and encourage you. Karna found support in Duryodhana, which played a crucial role in his journey. Build a network of mentors, peers, and friends who can provide guidance, motivation, and practical help.

Case Study: Overcoming Barriers in the Professional World

Consider the story of Maya, an ambitious young engineer who faced significant barriers in her career due to gender bias in her industry. Despite her qualifications and skills, she was often overlooked for promotions and key projects. Determined to break these barriers, Maya set clear career goals and developed a strategic plan.

She sought mentorship from successful women in her field, attended workshops to enhance her skills, and built a strong professional network. Maya also practiced resilience by staying focused on her goals despite setbacks. Over time, her efforts paid off—she secured a leadership position and became a role model for other women in engineering.

Research Findings: The Role of Resilience in Achieving Success

Research has shown that resilience is a critical factor in achieving long- term success. A study published in the Journal of Applied Psychology found that individuals with high levels of resilience are more likely to persevere through challenges and achieve their goals. Resilience enables individuals to adapt to changing circumstances and maintain their motivation despite difficulties.

Staying Focused and Encouraged

You've made remarkable progress on your journey of self-discovery and ambition. Breaking barriers can be challenging but remember to celebrate your achievements and stay focused on your goals. Here are some tips to stay encouraged:

- **Celebrate Your Progress:** Reflect on the barriers you've overcome and the steps you've taken towards unleashing your potential.
- **Stay Connected:** Continue engaging with your support system. Share your successes and challenges with them.
- **Set SMART Goals:** Define specific, measurable, achievable, relevant, and time-bound goals that align with your ambitions.
- **Create an Action Plan**: Develop a detailed plan to address each barrier, including the steps, resources, and support systems you need.
- **Cultivate Resilience:** Practice resilience by staying positive, learning from setbacks, and maintaining a growth mindset.
- **Build Your Support Network:** Identify mentors, peers, and friends who can provide guidance and encouragement.

As we conclude this chapter, remember that breaking barriers and unleashing your true potential is a journey that requires determination, resilience, and support. By drawing inspiration from Karna's unwavering commitment to his goals, you can navigate the obstacles in your path and achieve your dreams. In the next chapter, we will explore how to rise above limitations and maintain persistence, inspired by Karna's relentless pursuit of excellence. Let's continue this transformative journey together.

Turn the page, and let's explore how to rise above limitations and maintain persistence, drawing inspiration from Karna's remarkable journey.

◆◆◆

Chapter 10

Rising Above Limitations: Karna's Guide to Persistence

"*Success is not final, failure is not fatal: It is the courage to continue that counts.*"

- Winston Churchill

In the prior chapter, we discussed ways to recognize and conquer the obstacles hindering your ability to reach your full potential. Through establishing precise objectives, creating an actionable plan, fostering resilience, and seeking assistance, you have initiated the process of overcoming those challenges. I trust you have found the Barrier-Breaking Tips beneficial and are beginning to observe the favorable effects of these approaches in your life.

Karna inspires one with the Persistence Quotient. Despite several odds and handicaps forced by society on this born warrior, he refused to give up on excellence. There are innumerable instances in the journey of this central character when his sheer will and single-minded focus helped him transcend limitations.

One of the most inspiring examples of Karna's grit comes in the form of the pursuit of excellence in archery. Even when cursed by his teacher Parashurama, Karna did not give up. He persisted with this art and the desire to prove himself to reach his potential, which made him a relentless practiser and helped him become one of its greatest archers.

The story of Karna reminds us that the key lies in overcoming limitations with persistence toward achieving greatness. His journey teaches that with sheer determination and hard work, all obstacles are crossed.

How to Maintain Persistence and Rise Above Limitations

Rising above limitations requires unwavering persistence and a resilient mindset. Here are some steps to help you maintain persistence and overcome the challenges in your path:

1. **Set Long-Term and Short-Term Goals:** Setting both long-term and short-term goals helps maintain focus and motivation. Long-term goals provide direction, while short-term goals offer immediate targets to strive for. Karna's long-term goal was to become the greatest archer, while his short-term goals included mastering specific techniques and winning competitions.
2. **Break Down Tasks:** Break down your larger goals into smaller, manageable tasks. This makes the process less overwhelming and allows you to celebrate small victories along the way. Karna broke down his training into specific skills and techniques, mastering each one step by step.
3. **Develop a Routine:** Establishing a routine helps build consistency and discipline. Create a daily or weekly schedule that includes dedicated time for working

towards your goals. Karna's rigorous training regimen was a key factor in his success.

4. **Stay Positive and Focused:** Maintaining a positive mindset is crucial for persistence. Stay focused on your goals and remind yourself of your progress and achievements. Karna's unwavering focus and positive outlook helped him stay motivated despite setbacks.
5. **Embrace Failure as a Learning Opportunity:** View failures as opportunities to learn and grow. Each setback provides valuable lessons that can help you improve and move closer to your goals. Karna learned from his failures and used them as stepping stones to success.

Case Study: Persistence in Overcoming Professional Challenges

Consider the story of Jane, a software engineer who faced numerous setbacks in her career due to a lack of resources and support. Despite these challenges, Jane set clear goals for her professional development and broke them down into achievable tasks. She established a daily routine that included learning new skills, networking with industry professionals, and applying for better opportunities.

Jane's persistence paid off. Over time, she secured a position at a leading tech company and continued to advance her career. Her story illustrates the importance of setting goals, developing a routine, and embracing failure as a learning opportunity.

Research Findings: The Role of Persistence in Success

Research has shown that persistence is a critical factor in achieving long- term success. A study published in the Journal of Personality and Social Psychology found that individuals who exhibit high levels of persistence are more likely to achieve their goals, regardless of the challenges they face. Persistence enables individuals to stay motivated and focused, even in the face of setbacks.

Staying Focused and Encouraged

You've made incredible progress on your journey of self-discovery and ambition. Rising above limitations requires persistence and resilience, but remember to celebrate your achievements and stay focused on your goals.

Here are some tips to stay encouraged:

- **Celebrate Your Progress:** Reflect on the limitations you've overcome and the steps you've taken towards your goals.
- **Stay Connected:** Continue engaging with your support system. Share your successes and challenges with them.
- **Set Daily Goals:** Identify daily tasks that align with your larger goals and create a schedule to accomplish them.
- **Track Your Progress:** Regularly review your progress and celebrate small victories along the way.
- **Stay Positive:** Practice positive self-talk and focus on your achievements to stay motivated.
- **Learn from Failures:** Reflect on setbacks and identify lessons that can help you improve and move forward.

As we conclude this chapter, remember that rising above limitations requires unwavering persistence and a resilient mindset. By drawing inspiration from Karna's relentless pursuit of excellence, you can navigate the challenges in your path and achieve your goals. In the next chapter, we will explore the power of self-belief and how to build and maintain confidence, inspired by Karna's journey. Let's continue this transformative journey together.

Turn the page, and let's dive into the next chapter, where we'll explore the power of self-belief and how to build and maintain confidence, drawing inspiration from Karna's remarkable journey.

♦♦♦

Chapter 11

The Power of Self-Belief: Karna's Key to Success

"Believe in yourself and all that you are. Know that there is something inside you that is greater than any obstacle."

- Christian D. Larson

In the previous chapter, we explored the importance of persistence in overcoming limitations. By setting clear goals, breaking down tasks, developing a routine, maintaining a positive mindset, and embracing failure as a learning opportunity, you've learned how to rise above obstacles and stay focused on your journey.

The journey of Karna was not about breaking through the apparent barriers of the outside world or persisting in the face of ordeals but about self-realization. Though rejected by everyone and pressured by society's perception questioning his talents, Karna believed strongly in himself. This self-belief was the cornerstone of his success.

One such classic case of his great self-belief is the fact that he went to the archery event, knowing that he would be up against Arjuna himself, one of the most terrific archers. All say that Karna is perfect in his skills since he proves that by being at the top and surpasses all his opponents. All this self-belief was not overconfidence but a belief in his skills and the potential he holds in his heart toward his dream.

Karna's journey is enlightening; it is true that self-belief is such a strong force that can let us achieve greatness in life. His story inspires us to trust in our capabilities and to face everything life has in store for us with courage.

How to Build and Maintain Self-Belief

Building and maintaining self-belief is crucial for achieving success. Here are some steps to help you cultivate and strengthen your self-belief:

1. **Acknowledge Your Achievements:** Take time to recognize and celebrate your accomplishments, no matter how small they may seem. Reflecting on your successes helps reinforce your belief in your abilities. Karna celebrated his victories, using them as reminders of his potential.
2. **Surround Yourself with Positive Influences:** Surround yourself with people who believe in you and support your goals. Positive influences can boost your confidence and provide encouragement during challenging times. Karna found support in Duryodhana, who believed in his abilities and potential.
3. **Practice Positive Self-Talk:** Replace negative thoughts with positive affirmations. Remind yourself of your strengths and capabilities. Positive self-talk can help shift your mindset and reinforce your self-belief. Karna's inner dialogue was filled with determination and confidence.

4. **Set Realistic and Achievable Goals:** Set goals that are challenging yet attainable. Achieving these goals reinforces your belief in your abilities and motivates you to pursue even greater challenges. Karna set ambitious yet realistic goals, steadily progressing towards mastery.
5. **Learn from Failures:** View failures as opportunities to learn and grow. Each setback provides valuable lessons that can help you improve and strengthen your self-belief. Karna learned from his failures, using them as stepping stones to greater success.

Case Study: Building Self-Belief in Professional Life

Consider the story of Raj, a young entrepreneur who struggled with self-doubt after facing several business failures. Determined to overcome his insecurities, Raj began by acknowledging his past achievements and celebrating his successes, no matter how small. He surrounded himself with mentors and peers who believed in his vision and provided positive reinforcement.

Raj also practiced positive self-talk, replacing negative thoughts with affirmations of his capabilities. He set realistic and achievable goals, breaking down his larger vision into manageable steps. Despite setbacks, Raj viewed each failure as a learning opportunity, continually improving his strategies. Over time, his self-belief grew stronger, leading to the successful launch of his business.

Research Findings: The Impact of Self-Belief on Success

Research has consistently shown that self-belief is a critical factor in achieving success. A study published in the Journal of Applied Psychology found that individuals with high levels of self-belief are more likely to set challenging goals, persevere through difficulties, and achieve their objectives. Self-belief enhances motivation, resilience, and overall performance, making it a key determinant of success.

You've made incredible progress on your journey of self-discovery and ambition. Building and maintaining self-belief is essential for achieving your goals but remember to celebrate your achievements and stay focused on your path. Here are some tips to stay encouraged:

1. **Celebrate Your Progress:** Reflect on the self-belief you've cultivated and the steps you've taken towards your goals.
2. **Stay Connected:** Continue engaging with your support system. Share your successes and challenges with them.
3. **Practice Positive Self-Talk:** Replace negative thoughts with positive affirmations of your capabilities.
4. **Set Achievable Goals:** Define realistic and attainable goals that challenge you and reinforce your self-belief.
5. **Learn from Failures:** Reflect on past failures and identify the lessons they provide to improve and grow.

As we conclude this chapter, remember that self-belief is a powerful force that can drive you to achieve greatness. By drawing inspiration from Karna's unwavering confidence in his abilities, you can cultivate and maintain a strong belief in yourself, regardless of the challenges you face. In the next chapter, we will explore the balance between ambition and morality, and how to pursue your dreams without compromising your values, inspired by Karna's journey. Let's continue this transformative journey together.

Turn the page, and let's dive into the next chapter, where we'll explore the balance between ambition and morality, and how to pursue your dreams without compromising your values, drawing inspiration from Karna's remarkable journey.

◆◆◆

Chapter 12

Ambition vs. Morality: Walking Karna's Path

"Ambition is like love, impatient both of delays and rivals."

- Sir John Denham

In the previous chapter, we focused on the importance of empathy, open communication, setting boundaries, seeking mediation, and forgiveness in resolving family conflicts and healing past wounds. Remember, the strength of your family relationships can be a powerful support as you pursue your personal ambitions.

Karna's life was a constant tug-of-war between his ambitions and his moral compass. Born with the potential to be a great warrior, Karna faced numerous obstacles due to his social status. Despite these challenges, his ambition drove him to become one of the most skilled archers of his time. However, his path was fraught with moral dilemmas.

One of the most significant conflicts Karna faced was his loyalty to Duryodhana versus his knowledge of the righteousness of the Pandava's cause. Despite knowing that Duryodhana's actions were often morally questionable, Karna remained loyal due to his sense of gratitude and honor. This internal conflict between his ambition to prove himself and his moral obligations presents a valuable lesson on the delicate balance between achieving our goals and staying true to our values.

Balancing Ambition and Morality

Balancing ambition and morality is a challenge many of us face. Ambition drives us to achieve great things, but it should not come at the expense of our ethical principles. Here are some steps to help you navigate this balance:

1. **Define Your Ethical Boundaries:** Clearly define what you consider to be ethical and unethical behavior. This will serve as your moral compass when pursuing your ambitions. Karna's unwavering principles guided his decisions, even when faced with difficult choices.
2. **Align Your Goals with Your Values:** Ensure that your goals are aligned with your core values. This alignment will help you pursue your ambitions without compromising your integrity. Karna's ambition was always tempered by his commitment to honor and loyalty.
3. **Reflect on Potential Consequences:** Consider the potential consequences of your actions on both your personal integrity and those around you. Reflecting on the broader impact of your decisions can help you make more balanced choices.
4. **Seek Guidance and Mentorship:** Seek advice from trusted mentors or advisors who share your values. Their perspectives can provide valuable insights and help you stay grounded in your principles while pursuing your ambitions.

5. **Practice Self-Reflectio:** Regularly reflect on your actions and decisions to ensure they align with your ethical boundaries. Self-reflection allows you to stay true to your values and make adjustments as needed.

Case Study: Navigating Ambition in the Corporate World

Consider the story of a young executive named Alex who faced a moral dilemma in his career. Alex was offered a significant promotion that required him to engage in practices he felt were ethically questionable. Despite the allure of the promotion, Alex chose to decline the offer, prioritizing his integrity over immediate career advancement.

Instead, Alex sought a position that aligned with his values, even though it meant starting over in a new company. Over time, his commitment to his principles earned him respect and led to a leadership role where he could drive change without compromising his ethics.

Alex's story illustrates the importance of staying true to one's values while pursuing professional ambitions.

Research Findings: The Impact of Ethical Leadership

Research has shown that ethical leadership leads to higher levels of trust, employee satisfaction, and organizational performance. A study published in the Journal of Business Ethics found that leaders who prioritize ethical behavior foster a positive work environment and are more likely to achieve long-term success. This demonstrates that balancing ambition with morality is not only the right thing to do but also beneficial for sustainable achievement.

Personal Experience: Balancing Ambition and Morality

In my own journey as an author, I faced numerous opportunities that promised quick success but required compromising my values. One particular instance involved a lucrative publishing deal that demanded altering the message of my book to fit a more commercial narrative. After much reflection, I chose to stay true to my original vision, even though it meant forgoing the deal. This decision ultimately led to a deeper connection with my readers and long-term success built on authenticity and trust.

As we conclude this chapter, remember that balancing ambition and morality is crucial for achieving sustainable success and maintaining your integrity. By drawing inspiration from Karna's unwavering principles, you can navigate the complexities of your ambitions while staying true to your values. In the next section, we will explore the role of resilience and redemption in overcoming life's challenges and achieving personal growth, inspired by Karna's remarkable journey. Let's continue this transformative journey together.

Turn the page, and let's dive into the next section, where we'll explore the power of resilience and redemption, and how to overcome life's challenges to achieve personal growth, drawing inspiration from Karna's inspiring story.

♦♦♦

Section 4

Resilience and Redemption: How to Turn Adversity into Triumph Without Losing Hope Even If You've Faced Injustice Congratulations on making it this far!

You've shown incredible dedication and resilience by navigating the complexities of self-discovery, building healthy relationships, balancing ambition with morality, and fostering self-belief. You've implemented the strategies, seen some quick wins, and have a clearer understanding of where you are in your journey. Now, as we move into the final stretch, it's time to focus on resilience and redemption—how to turn adversity into triumph and maintain hope, even in the face of injustice.

In this final section of the book, we'll delve into the transformative power of resilience and redemption. Inspired by Karna's remarkable journey, we'll explore how to build emotional strength, overcome injustices, and find growth in adversity. These final chapters are designed to guide you towards personal victory, ensuring that every struggle you face becomes a stepping stone to greater success and fulfilment.

You've already demonstrated amazing resilience and dedication by making it this far. The insights and tools in the following chapters will empower you to navigate life's adversities with strength and grace, ensuring that your journey towards victory is not just possible but inevitable.

Let's embark on the last phase of this profound journey with me. A superior you is merely a couple of pages ahead. Let's persist in converting each obstacle into a chance for advancement and every disappointment into progress.

Turn the page, and let's commence Chapter 13, delving into strategies to cultivate resilience and conquer adversities, drawing inspiration from Karna's resolute resolve and fortitude.

Chapter 13

Overcoming Injustice: Karna's Path to Resilience

"The greatest glory in living lies not in never falling, but in rising every time we fall."

- Nelson Mandela

In the previous chapter, we explored discovering your purpose and aligning your actions with your core values. You were prompted to contemplate your passions and establish significant objectives. Before progressing, confirm you have made efforts to recognize and follow your purpose.

Karna's life was nothing short of ruthless adversity and injustice. From an unknown parentage, which denied him his rightful place, to these vicious tides of karma in the form of curses from people who derogated him at every turn, Karna's life is a long-drawn sequence of mishaps that would have broken many spirits. But nothing could subdue his spirit and will to rise above all these injustices.

One of the most striking examples of Karna's resilience was his reaction to being rejected from participating in the royal archery tournament on account of his social status. Rather than give way to despair, Korna approached Parashurama—who was considered second to none as a teacher of martial arts—and became truly adept at archery under his tutelage. Even after he had been cursed by Parashurama upon the latter's discovery of who he really was, Karn continued to train incessantly and never allowed these wrongs to define him.

Karna's story shows us how much resilience to rise above the injustices perpetrated against us and to use them as fuel that will drive us toward our goals. Indeed, his journey does very strongly put forward the fact that though we may not be able to change the circumstances, we can definitely stem the response.

"Injustice anywhere is a threat to justice everywhere."

- Martin Luther King Jr.

Building Resilience to Overcome Injustice

Overcoming injustice requires a resilient mindset and the courage to stand up for oneself. Resilience is the ability to bounce back from adversity and keep moving forward despite challenges. Here are some steps to help you build resilience and overcome injustices in your own life:

1. **Acknowledge Your Feelings:** Allow yourself to feel the emotions that come with facing injustice. Acknowledging these feelings is the first step towards healing and building resilience. Karna did not shy away from his emotions; instead, he used them as motivation to prove his worth.

2. **Focus on What You Can Control:** While you cannot control the actions of others or the injustices you face, you can control your response to them. Focus on what you can do to improve your situation and take proactive steps towards your goals. Karna focused on mastering his skills despite the societal limitations placed on him.
3. **Seek Support:** Surround yourself with a supportive network of friends, family, and mentors who can provide encouragement and guidance. Karna found support in Duryodhana, who recognized his potential and stood by him. Having a strong support system can help you stay resilient in the face of adversity.
4. **Develop a Positive Mindset:** Cultivate a positive mindset by focusing on your strengths and the progress you've made. Practice gratitude and remind yourself of the things you are grateful for. Karna's positive outlook and determination helped him stay motivated despite numerous setbacks.
5. **Learn and Grow from Adversity:** View adversity as an opportunity for growth. Reflect on the lessons you can learn from the challenges you face and use them to become stronger and more resilient. Karna's ability to learn from his experiences and grow as a warrior was a key factor in his resilience.

Case Study

A notable case study is the story of Malala Yousafzai, who faced extreme injustice when she was shot by the Taliban for advocating girls' education in Pakistan. Despite the life-threatening attack, Malala continued her fight for education and became the youngest-ever Nobel Prize laureate. Her resilience and unwavering commitment to justice inspire millions worldwide.

Case Study: Overcoming Injustice in Personal Life

Priya Sharma had this dream of becoming a successful entrepreneur since she was a small child. She did everything she could to get her business established, but in the final stages of her success, she fell on hard times. Priya became the victim of a very unfair accusation from a big businessman who wanted to take her out of the competition, hence, she was charged with breaking a contract. The court battle that followed not only involved legal complexity but also sapped her emotionally and financially.

Priya, on the other hand, has refused to be tarnished by this wrongdoing. She demonstrated her capabilities to her superiors through the method she employed at work, and she left a professional and legal imprint that will never be forgotten. She enhanced her group, renovated her business, focused on the standards of difficult work and advanced to do as such. Priya quickly changed the negative feedback into something positive that talks about a phoenix's perseverance and story of survival.

Times went by and Priya's efforts finally bore fruit. She won the lawsuit, which made her even stronger than she had been before. The business she established soon became a popular and cloaked in impressive fantasy in which success took her to heights she never imagined. Behind the scenes, Priya's odyssey addresses the victory of the more significant standards of strength and the need to express no to shamefulness, regardless of how troublesome it is.

Research Findings: The Impact of Resilience on Success

Research has shown that resilience is a key factor in achieving long- term success. A study published in the Journal of Positive Psychology found that individuals with high levels of resilience are more likely to overcome challenges and achieve their goals. Resilience helps individuals adapt to changing circumstances, maintain a positive outlook, and stay motivated despite setbacks.

You've made great progress on your path to resilience and self- exploration. As we wrap up this section, keep in mind that fostering resilience is vital for conquering adversity and attaining your aspirations. By mirroring Karna's resolute resolve and fortitude, you can confront hurdles head-on and triumph. In the upcoming segment, we will delve into converting setbacks into opportunities for growth and cultivating resilience from difficulties, drawing lessons from Karna's exceptional odyssey. Let's continue this transformative journey together.

Turn the page, and let's dive into the next chapter, where we'll explore how to forge strength from adversity and achieve personal growth, drawing inspiration from Karna's inspiring story.

◆◆◆

Chapter 14

Forging Strength: Turning Adversity into Growth

"Strength does not come from winning. Your struggles develop your strengths. When you go through hardships and decide not to surrender, that is strength."

- Arnold Schwarzenegger

In the previous chapter, we explored the importance of resilience in overcoming injustices. We discussed how to acknowledge your feelings, focus on what you can control, seek support, develop a positive mindset, and learn from adversity. I hope you've found the Resilience Building Workbook useful and have started to see the benefits of these practices in your life.

Karna's life was a continuous journey of facing and overcoming adversity. Despite the numerous injustices and challenges he faced, Karna used these experiences to grow stronger and more determined. His ability to turn adversity into a source of strength is one of the most inspiring aspects of his story.

One of the most significant moments of growth for Karna was his acceptance of his true lineage. Instead of allowing the revelation to shatter his self-worth, Karna chose to embrace his identity and continue fighting for his place in the world. This acceptance, combined with his relentless pursuit of excellence, allowed him to grow into one of the most formidable warriors of his time.

Karna's journey teaches us that adversity, when faced with the right mindset, can become a powerful catalyst for growth. His story is a testament to the fact that our struggles can shape us into stronger, more resilient individuals.

Turning Adversity into Growth

Adversity can be a powerful catalyst for personal growth if approached with the right mindset. Here are some steps to help you turn your struggles into strengths:

1. **Embrace Challenges as Opportunities:** View challenges as opportunities for growth rather than obstacles. Embracing adversity with a positive mindset allows you to learn and grow from your experiences. Karna saw each challenge as a chance to prove himself and improve his skills.
2. **Reflect on Your Experiences:** Take time to reflect on your experiences and the lessons they offer. Reflecting on adversity helps you gain insights into your strengths and areas for improvement. Karna's reflections on his challenges helped him develop resilience and determination.
3. **Set Growth-Oriented Goals:** Set goals that focus on personal growth and development. These goals should challenge you to step out of your comfort zone and push your limits. Karna's ambition to become a master archer was a growth-oriented goal that drove him to overcome numerous obstacles.

4. **Cultivate a Growth Mindset:** Adopt a growth mindset by believing that your abilities and intelligence can be developed through hard work and dedication. This mindset encourages you to embrace challenges and persist in the face of setbacks. Karna's growth mindset was evident in his relentless pursuit of excellence.
5. **Seek Learning Opportunities:** Actively seek out opportunities to learn and grow from your experiences. This could involve seeking feedback, attending workshops, or engaging in self-study. Karna's decision to learn from Parashurama, despite the challenges, exemplifies the importance of seeking learning opportunities.

Case Study: Growth Through Adversity in Personal Life

Arjun Patel suffered a life-changing event when he was struck by a terrible accident that injured him and made him go through surgeries. He faced not only the bodily pain but also the depression and mental stress of his mind. He was originally a very active person who used to be outdoors for most of the day which was overnight replaced with being in a hospital bed and a body which was in much pain the whole period of recovery. Instead of feeling beaten, Arjun decided to take this challenge as an opportunity to grow.

He went through long sessions of exercises and thoughts about the relationships and objects he valued. He came to realize that writing had become a means of the outlet of his thoughts and feelings. The Healing process he underwent became the process of self-realization.

Arjun ended up starting a blog with the goal of not only telling his story but also being there to inspire and support anyone who faces similar challenges. His essay was something that made people remember it and the way he confronted his personal adversity with upbeatness became the source of encouragement and inspiration for countless readers.

Gradually he recovered from his physical infirmity, through his new mission, he found his spiritual wellness. It's a role he assumed to champion resilience and positive thinking, confirming that real growth comes from the most challenging experiences.

Research Findings: The Benefits of a Growth Mindset

Research has shown that individuals with a growth mindset are more likely to overcome adversity and achieve their goals. A study published in the Journal of Personality and Social Psychology found that individuals who believe their abilities can be developed through effort and learning are more resilient and adaptable. This mindset helps individuals view challenges as opportunities for growth, leading to greater success and fulfilment.

As we conclude this chapter, remember that turning adversity into growth is a powerful way to achieve personal development and success.

By drawing inspiration from Karna's resilience and growth through challenges, you can navigate your own adversities and emerge stronger and more determined. In the final chapter, we will explore the themes of redemption and forgiveness, and how to find peace and fulfillment through these transformative processes. Let's continue this transformative journey together.

Turn the page, and let's dive into the final chapter, where we'll explore the power of redemption and forgiveness, and how to achieve personal growth and fulfilment, drawing inspiration from Karna's remarkable legacy.

♦♦♦

Chapter 15

Redemption and Forgiveness: Karna's Legacy

"Forgiveness is the fragrance that the violet sheds on the heel that has crushed it."

- Mark Twain

In the previous chapter, we explored how to turn adversity into growth. We discussed the importance of embracing challenges, reflecting on experiences, setting growth-oriented goals, cultivating a growth mindset, and seeking learning opportunities. I hope you've found the Growth Mindset Guide useful and have started to see the benefits of approaching challenges with a positive mindset.

Karna's life was a journey marked by struggles, resilience, and ultimately, a quest for redemption. Despite his unwavering loyalty to Duryodhana and his role in the Kurukshetra war, Karna's heart was filled with a longing for acceptance and forgiveness. One of the most poignant moments in his story is his final encounter with his mother, Kunti.

When Kunti revealed Karna's true lineage, it was a moment of profound realization for him. He chose to forgive her for abandoning him, understanding the complexities of her situation. This act of forgiveness not only brought him peace but also showcased his immense strength of character. Karna's story teaches us that forgiveness, both of oneself and others, is a powerful force that can lead to profound healing and redemption.

The Power of Redemption and Forgiveness

Redemption and forgiveness are transformative processes that allow us to heal from past wounds and move forward with a sense of peace and fulfillment. Here are some steps to help you embrace forgiveness and seek redemption:

1. **Acknowledge Your Mistakes:** The first step towards redemption is to acknowledge your mistakes and take responsibility for your actions. Reflect on the past and identify areas where you could have acted differently. Karna acknowledged his role in the Kurukshetra war and sought to make peace with his actions.
2. **Seek Forgiveness:** Seek forgiveness from those you have wronged. This process requires humility and a sincere desire to make amends. Karna's forgiveness of Kunti was a crucial step in his journey towards redemption.
3. **Forgive Yourself:** Self-forgiveness is essential for healing and moving forward. Acknowledge your mistakes, learn from them, and give yourself permission to let go of guilt and regret. Karna's ability to forgive himself for his past actions allowed him to find peace.
4. **Make Amends:** Take actionable steps to make amends for your mistakes. This could involve apologizing, making reparations, or taking corrective actions. Karna's dedication to his principles and his efforts to make peace with his past were part of his redemption journey.

5. **Cultivate Compassion:** Cultivate compassion for yourself and others. Understand that everyone makes mistakes and that forgiveness is a path to healing and growth. Karna's compassion for Kunti and his brothers exemplified his strength and character.

Case Study: Personal Redemption and Forgiveness

One wrong move changed Radhika Singh's life overnight and now has her closest friends, and family members at odds with who she is. The shame and regret were almost more than she could bear as the weight of her actions settled deep into this young woman. Radhika knew she had wronged and needed to make things right.

To cleanse the shame that weighed so heavily on her soul, her path of redemption led through confession and reconciliation with those she had wronged. Radhika focused on self-growth and made herself a better person. She went to therapy, support groups, and began doing volunteer work with people who were having similar difficulties.

With the help of the organization, Radhika learned the true meaning of forgiveness, not from others, but from herself. She started over her relations step by step and proved her genuinely committed change through her actions. The major change she underwent was so deep that it made her family members trust her again and found new respect from those who had witnessed her journey.

"To err is human, to forgive, divine."

- Alexander Pope

The case of Radhika suggests that there can be a way to change if a person is devoted and willing to change. She has acquired both forgiveness and personal growth and that has, in turn, encouraged other people to believe in those whom everybody still can't see through the glass to the authentic person outside.

Research Findings: The Benefits of Forgiveness

Research has shown that forgiveness is associated with numerous psychological benefits, including reduced stress, improved mental health, and increased well-being. A study published in the Journal of Behavioral Medicine found that individuals who practice forgiveness experience lower levels of anxiety and depression, and higher levels of life satisfaction. Forgiveness promotes emotional healing and fosters healthier relationships.

Next Steps: 21-Day Redemption and Forgiveness Challenge

To help you embrace forgiveness and seek redemption, here is a 21-day challenge you can start right away:

Week 1: Acknowledge and Reflect

- **Day 1-3:** Reflect on past mistakes and acknowledge your role in them.
- **Day 4-7:** Write down your reflections and identify areas where you could have acted differently.

Week 2: Seek Forgiveness and Make Amends

- **Day 8-10:** Reach out to those you have wronged and seek their forgiveness.
- **Day 11-14:** Take actionable steps to make amends for your mistakes.

Week 3: Forgive Yourself and Cultivate Compassion

- **Day 15-17:** Practice self-forgiveness through reflection and positive affirmations.

- **Day 18-21**: Cultivate compassion for yourself and others by engaging in acts of kindness and understanding.

As we conclude this final chapter, remember that redemption and forgiveness are powerful steps towards healing and personal growth. By drawing inspiration from Karna's remarkable journey, you can navigate your own path to redemption and find peace and fulfilment.

Thank you for taking this journey with me. Your commitment to self- improvement and growth is truly inspiring. Remember, each step you take brings you closer to becoming the best version of yourself.

Turn the page, and let's embark on this final journey of redemption and forgiveness, drawing strength and inspiration from Karna's legacy.

♦♦♦

Conclusion

Embracing Your Inner Karna - A Life Lived with Purpose

As we reach the conclusion of this transformative journey, it's essential to reflect on the broader implications of Karna's story and the lessons we've uncovered. Throughout this book, we've delved deep into Karna's life, extracting timeless wisdom and practical strategies to help you unleash your inner warrior and transform struggles into strengths.

Why should we care about Karna's legacy? Because it transcends time, culture, and circumstance, offering us a roadmap for navigating life's challenges with resilience, integrity, and grace. Karna's story is a testament to the human spirit's capacity for growth, redemption, and triumph over adversity. By internalizing his lessons, you join a larger conversation about courage, determination, and the pursuit of a meaningful life.

What do we do now with the wisdom we've gained? It's time to take actionable steps to apply Karna's teachings to our lives. Here are some practical tips to guide you:

1. ***Embrace Your Unique Identity:*** *Celebrate your individuality and use it as a source of strength. Reflect on what makes you*

unique and how you can leverage those qualities to overcome obstacles.

2. ***Face Rejection Head-On:*** *View rejection not as a setback but as a redirection. Use it as an opportunity to refine your skills and prove your worth, just as Karna did.*
3. ***Cultivate Resilience:*** *Build your resilience muscle by facing challenges with a positive mindset. Remember, resilience is about bouncing back stronger, not avoiding difficulties.*
4. ***Seek Support:*** *Surround yourself with a supportive network. Find friends, mentors, or communities that believe in you and provide the encouragement you need to keep moving forward.*
5. ***Focus on Self-Improvement:*** *Continuously invest in yourself. Identify areas for growth and take deliberate steps to enhance your skills and knowledge.*
6. ***Stay True to Your Values:*** *Let your values guide your decisions and actions. Even in the face of pressure, hold on to your principles and live authentically.*

As you continue your journey, remember that the path to self-discovery and empowerment is ongoing. Karna's legacy is not just a story from the past; it's a living testament to the potential within each of us. By embracing these teachings, you carry forward his legacy, becoming a beacon of resilience, strength, and authenticity.

In the words of Charles Darwin, "It is not the strongest of the species that survive, nor the most intelligent, but the one most responsive to change." Let Karna's story inspire you to live with purpose and make a positive impact in the world.

Take a moment to reflect on your journey so far. How has Karna's wisdom resonated with you? What steps will you take to integrate these lessons into your life? Remember, this is just the beginning. The true power of Karna's legacy lies in its application.

As you move forward, keep the spirit of Karna alive in your actions. Embrace your inner warrior, face challenges with courage, and live a life that reflects the strength, wisdom, and resilience you've discovered within yourself. The journey doesn't end here; it evolves with each step you take, each challenge you overcome, and each triumph you achieve.

Thank you for embarking on this journey with me. May Karna's legacy inspire you to unleash your full potential and live a life of purpose and fulfilment. Keep moving forward, and remember, you have the power to rewrite your story and shape your destiny.

With heartfelt gratitude,

Isha Gangrade

Books by this Author

King Raavan: Beyond the Myths, Unveiling a Noble Legacy

Step into the world of ancient Sri Lanka, where legends intertwine with reality, and the story of a misunderstood ruler comes to light. This captivating journey, "King Raavan: Beyond the Myth - Unveiling a Noble Legacy," transcends the boundaries of folklore, revealing the human tale beneath the mythical veneer.

Join the enigmatic Raavan from his formative years, profoundly influenced by Sri Lanka's rich cultural heritage, to his ascent to kingship marked by challenges that shaped not only his reign but also the essence of his character. Discover a ruler whose leadership is not about the superficial display of power, but is rooted in the welfare of his people, economic prosperity, and social justice.

This narrative goes beyond politics to explore the personal dimensions of Raavan's life—depicting him as a father, friend, and complex individual. It is a story of triumphs and trials, compassion and ambition, where Raavan's legacy is portrayed in shades of light and dark.

The final section brings Raavan's story to a resonant conclusion, echoing in the corridors of our minds. Yet, the journey does not end here. Look forward to the next installment, where we will delve into the life of Suryaputra Karna. His saga promises to captivate your imagination. Raavan's tale is complete, but new stories await on the horizon. Prepare to be enthralled as the journey continues.

This book became an Amazon bestseller in all three categories, a testament to its powerful storytelling and the timeless allure of its subject.

Praise for Author

About "King Raavan: Beyond the Myths, Unveiling a Noble Legacy"

"A riveting exploration of one of history's most misunderstood figures. Isha Gangrade breathes new life into the ancient myths, providing a fresh perspective that captivates from start to finish. A must-read!"

— Priya Sharma, Author of "Timeless Tales"

"Gangrade's debut is nothing short of a masterpiece. Her meticulous research and compelling storytelling make 'King Raavan' a standout work in the genre of historical mythologies."

— Rohan Mehta, Literary Critic and Blogger

"Isha Gangrade has a unique talent for weaving complex characters with deep emotional resonance. 'King Raavan' is a testament to her ability to transform myth into relatable, human stories."

— Sneha Kapoor, Editor at Mythic Reads

"An insightful and transformative read. Gangrade's portrayal of Raavan challenges traditional narratives and offers a thought-provoking journey into his noble legacy."

— Anita Desai, Book Reviewer and Historian

About "10 Arrows of Wisdom: Unleashing Your Inner Warrior"

"In '10 Arrows of Wisdom,' Isha Gangrade brilliantly distills the essence of Karna's journey, offering practical wisdom for modern readers. Her writing is both enlightening and empowering."

— Arjun Patel, Author of "Ancient Paths to Modern Success"

"Isha Gangrade's '10 Arrows of Wisdom' is a guidebook for anyone seeking to transform their struggles into strengths. Her insightful reflections on Karna's story are deeply inspiring."

— Neha Verma, Personal Development Coach

"Gangrade seamlessly blends ancient wisdom with contemporary relevance. '10 Arrows of Wisdom' is a treasure trove of life lessons that resonate deeply with today's challenges."

— Ravi Kumar, Motivational Speaker

"Isha Gangrade's exploration of Karna's life is both profound and practical. '10 Arrows of Wisdom' is a beacon of light for those navigating their own paths of self-discovery and resilience."

— Kavita Rao, Founder of The Inner Strength Project

About the author

An MBA-HR professional currently working as a Quality Analyst. Her debut book, King Raavan: Beyond the Myths, Unveiling a Noble Legacy, became an Amazon bestseller.

The ancient myths have always held a special place in her heart. They're not just dusty tales; they're vibrant tapestries woven with lessons that resonate across time. Karna's story,

in particular, captivated her. Here was a warrior of immense talent, ostracized and underestimated. Yet, he rose above his circumstances, refusing to let his birth dictate his destiny.

But Karna's story isn't just about him. It's a mirror reflecting the struggles we all face: rejection, self-doubt, the yearning to forge our own path.

This book is her attempt to bridge the gap between ancient wisdom and modern challenges. By unpacking the "10 Arrows of Wisdom" hidden within Karna's journey, she hopes to empower readers to rewrite their own stories, transforming struggles into strengths and unleashing their inner warrior.

As a lover of language, she's fascinated by the power of stories to shape our lives. Each narrative, even a myth from millennia ago, can offer valuable lessons. In 10 Arrows of Wisdom, she explores how Karna's experiences connect to the challenges we face today. It's a journey of self-discovery, not just for the characters, but for us, the readers, as well.

Perhaps you've been knocked down by rejection or maybe self-doubt whispers in your ear. This book is for you. It's about learning from the past, embracing the power within you, and rewriting your story, one arrow at a time.

As a writer, she draws inspiration from personal experiences and the countless stories of ordinary people overcoming extraordinary challenges. These stories fueled her passion for 10 Arrows of Wisdom, serving as a constant reminder that we're not alone in this journey of life. And within the pages of this book, she hopes readers will find not just Karna's story, but a reflection of their strength and the potential to rewrite their destiny.

Connect with Isha on Instagram @ishag786 or email her at ishag.4ever@gmail.com or visit: ishagangrade.com to learn more about her work and join the journey of rewriting your story, one arrow at a time.